ROSEN ✓ *Verified*

CURRENT ISSUES

GENDER IDENTITY

Char Light

ROSEN
PUBLISHING

New York

Published in 2021 by The Rosen Publishing Group, Inc.
29 East 21st Street, New York, NY 10010

Editor: Amanda Vink
Book Design: Reann Nye

Photo Credits: Cover Westend61/Getty Images; series Art PinkPueblo/Shutterstock.com; p. 5 ROBYN BECK/AFP/Getty Images; p. 7 sashamolly/Shutterstock.com; p. 9 Time Life Pictures/The LIFE Picture Collection/Getty Images; p. 11 The Washington Post/Getty Images; p. 13 Hindustan Times/Getty Images; p. 15 Evgeniia Siiankovskaia/iStock/Getty Images Plus/Getty Images; p. 17 ullstein bild Dtl./ullstein bild/Getty Images; p. 21 Comstock/Stockbyte/Getty Images; p. 23 Emma McIntyre/Getty Images Entertainment/Getty Images; p. 25 Mike Pont/Getty Images Entertainment/Getty Images; p. 27 Rich Fury/Getty Images Entertainment/Getty Images; p. 29 Underwood Archives/Archive Photos/Getty Images; p. 31 Michael Ochs Archives/Getty Images; p. 33 Porter Gifford/RETIRED/Hulton Archive/Getty Images; p. 35 Santiago Felipe/Getty Images Entertainment/Getty Images; p. 36 Justin Sutcliffe/ASSOCIATED PRESS; p. 37 New York Daily News Archive/New York Daily News/Getty Images; p. 39 (Bagger) AFP/Getty Images; p. 39 (Saelua) Larry Busacca/Getty Images Entertainment/Getty Images; p. 39 (Mosier) Slaven Vlasic/Getty Images Entertainment/Getty Images; p. 39 (Jenner) Phillip Faraone/FilmMagic/Getty Images; p. 41 J. Bicking/Shutterstock.com; p. 43 Evan El-Amin/Shutterstock.com; p. 45 Rawpixel.com/Shutterstock.com.

Library of Congress Cataloging-in-Publication Data

Names: Light, Char, author.
Title: Gender identity / Char Light.
Description: New York : Rosen Publishing, [2021] | Series: Rosen verified: current issues
Identifiers: LCCN 2020000879 | ISBN 9781499468373 (paperback) | ISBN 9781499468380 (library binding)
Subjects: LCSH: Gender identity—Juvenile literature.
Classification: LCC HQ18.552 .L54 2021 | DDC 305.3—dc23
LC record available at https://lccn.loc.gov/2020000879

Manufactured in the United States of America

Some of the images in this book illustrate individuals who are models. The depictions do not imply actual situations or events.

CPSIA Compliance Information: Batch #BSR20. For Further Information contact Rosen Publishing, New York, New York at 1-800-237-9932.

Find us on

CONTENTS

GENDER IS MANY THINGS

Gender is something we experience, or feel. It's one of the ways society labels people and sets expectations for how people act. These labels drive how we go through the world.

Most people experience gender inside too. Everyone who feels gender experiences it in their own way. That's gender **identity**. There have always been people who experience their gender differently from how they were labeled.

The words we use to talk about gender have changed over time. They'll keep changing! Society's ideas about gender are changing too. More people are talking about their gender identities. Studies show that it helps people to live as the gender they feel. Activists are working to make society comfortable and safe for people of all gender identities.

✔ **VERIFIED**

For more information about International Transgender Day of Visibility, visit this website:
**https://www.hrc.org/resources/
international-transgender-day-of-visibility**

March 31 is International Transgender Day of Visibility. It's a day to celebrate transgender people, or those whose gender **assigned** at birth is different from how they feel. It's also a time to talk about the issues transgender people face.

THE GENDER BINARY

All **cultures** have their own ideas about gender. Throughout history, most cultures have recognized only two genders. These are female and male. This is called the gender binary.

The gender binary labels human bodies in only two ways. These two labels are based on different sex **traits**. Some sex traits are labeled female. Some are labeled male. In this system, babies are assigned a gender label. It's based on the sex traits they show at birth.

BIRTH CERTIFICATES

Your birth certificate is a paper you get from the government when you're born. It's a form of **identification** (ID). Birth certificates list a person's assigned sex. This is called a gender marker. Gender markers can also be found on passports and driver's licenses.

BOY OR GIRL?

A baby's gender, based on sex traits, is often assigned before birth. In the United States, historically, blue has been for boys and pink has been used for girls.

GENDER ROLES

Societies expect people to look and act a certain way. The **role** a person is expected to play in their society is often based on their gender label. This is called a gender role.

Gender roles change over time as society changes. This happened during World War II. Women often did not work outside the home before this time. During the war, however, society needed women to work because many men were in battle. Women even joined the military. After the war, women fought to keep working.

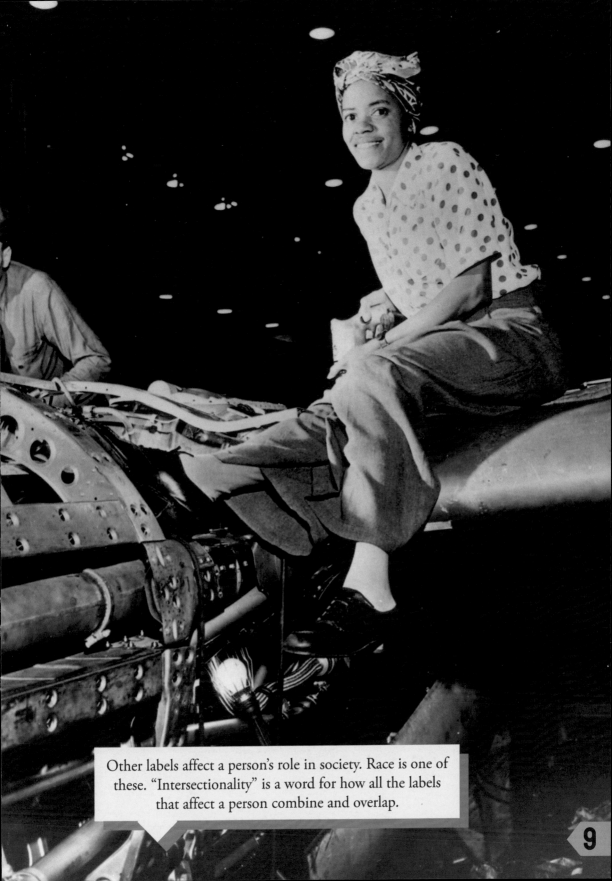

Other labels affect a person's role in society. Race is one of these. "Intersectionality" is a word for how all the labels that affect a person combine and overlap.

CULTURES BEYOND THE BINARY

Some cultures have more than two gender roles. The Bugis people in Indonesia have five genders. They also have three sexes. One of these genders is *bissu*. People who are *bissu* are a combination of all genders in Bugis culture. They are seen as powerful religious people. They often conduct services and act as a go-between for humans and spirits.

More than 155 Native American cultures have a gender identity belief called two-spirit. This identity is a cross between female and male gender roles. Two-spirit people are seen as special.

FAST FACT

MANY NATIVE AMERICAN CULTURES EACH HAVE THEIR OWN WORD FOR TWO-SPIRIT PEOPLE. "TWO-SPIRIT" BECAME A WORD IN 1990. IT'S AN UMBRELLA TERM FOR THESE NATIVE IDENTITIES.

Travis Goldtooth was Miss Montana Two-Spirit in 2019. They're shown here at the first Two-Spirit Powwow in Arizona. This is an event for Two-Spirit Native Americans.

India and nearby countries have a gender role called hijra. This is seen as a third gender. It describes many gender identities. Hijras experienced **discrimination**. Sadly, this continues today. The Supreme Court in India ruled in 2014 that people could be identified on official documents under this third gender group. Many people believe the laws need to go farther. They believe people should be protected from discrimination.

Colonization affected gender roles in India and in Native American cultures. The British colonizers forced these cultures to follow the gender binary. The good news is that things are changing. Today hijras and two-spirit people are recognized more.

WORDS AND GENDER

Some people don't use the word "hijra" today. They may identify by another term instead. Other people are proud to identify as hijra.

Laxmi Narayan Tripathi is one of the best-known gender activists in India. Tripathi identifies as hijra.

WHAT DOES SCIENCE SAY?

Scientists know that human bodies vary in a lot of ways. This includes our sex traits. Many sex traits don't fit the female or male labels humans have made up. For example, a person may be born with **ambiguous** sex organs. A person may have a different combination of **chromosomes** than what is often part of the gender binary. These sex traits are called intersex.

Intersex traits happen naturally. They aren't a problem. They're just one of the many ways humans are different. Scientists now know that sex traits come in a **spectrum**. This means there are more than two types of human bodies.

About 1.7 percent of babies in the United States are born with intersex traits. That's close to the number of people with red hair!

INTERSEX TRAITS

There are many different intersex traits. Most people with intersex traits are perfectly healthy.

Some people who have intersex traits don't find out until later in life. They may find out during puberty. This is a time when the human body goes through many changes. Some sex traits form during this time.

They may also find out if they try to have a baby. Intersex traits can affect this. Other people may never know they have intersex traits.

Erik Schinegger

Erik Schinegger is an Austrian skier. He was raised as a girl. He found out he was intersex in 1967. He wasn't allowed to ski in the Winter Olympics because of the discovery.

Schinegger lived as a man after a gender test. He changed his name from Erika to Erik. He made medical changes to his body. But he wasn't allowed to ski on Austria's team as a man or a woman.

INTERSEX RIGHTS

The gender binary creates **challenges** for many people with intersex traits. This can start at birth. Sometimes doctors make changes to a baby's body. They try to make it fit a female or male label. This kind of change isn't for the baby's health. It also isn't the baby's (or sometimes the parents') choice.

Intersex people can have other medical experiences that they do not choose. There have been cases where doctors have not given medical information to intersex people. Activists are trying to stop these kinds of things from happening.

OII Australia, an intersex rights activist group now called Intersex Human Rights Australia, made the intersex flag in 2013. The circle shows that intersex people are whole and complete.

INTERSEX ORGANIZATIONS AROUND THE WORLD

International
(more than one nation)

- ILGA World
- OutRight Action International
- ILGA Europe
- Intersex Asia

UK

- Intersex UK

Uganda

- Supportive Initiative for People with Atypical Sex Development

New Zealand

- Intersex Trust Aotearoa New Zealand

Taiwan

- Organization Intersex International Chinese

North America

- Intersex Campaign for Equality
- Intersex & Genderqueer
- Recognition Project Gender
- Intersex Justice Project
- Canadian Centre for Gender and Sexual Diversity

Kenya

- Intersex Persons Society of Kenya

South Africa

- Intersex South Africa

Australia

- Intersex Human Rights Australia

Argentina

- Global Action for Trans* Equality

INTERSEX AND GENDERS

Sex traits aren't the same thing as gender. In the gender binary, people assign a gender based on the sex traits a baby has. Females are girls. Males are boys.

Intersex traits don't fit these labels. But many intersex people are given a female or male label anyway. Some intersex people identify as the gender they are assigned. However, many identify as a different gender from their label. This can cause painful problems for them.

GENDER MARKERS ON IDs

Most IDs have gender markers. They usually must match the gender on a birth certificate. It can be very hard for people to get an ID that matches their identity.

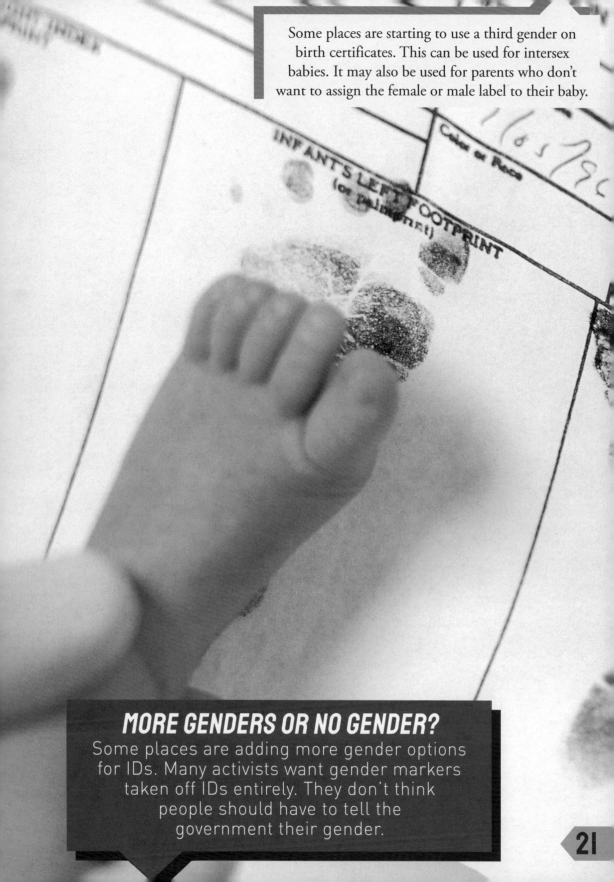

Some places are starting to use a third gender on birth certificates. This can be used for intersex babies. It may also be used for parents who don't want to assign the female or male label to their baby.

MORE GENDERS OR NO GENDER?

Some places are adding more gender options for IDs. Many activists want gender markers taken off IDs entirely. They don't think people should have to tell the government their gender.

GENDER IS A SPECTRUM

Scientists have found that your gender identity is based on more than your body. Gender is a spectrum.

Many people identify as the gender they were assigned at birth. People who feel this way are cisgender. But some people don't identify as the gender they were assigned at birth. Their gender identity doesn't match their assigned label. This big group of people is called the transgender community.

WHAT'S THE DIFFERENCE BETWEEN TRANSGENDER AND INTERSEX?

Transgender and intersex are different things. "Transgender" describes a person's gender identity. It's how they feel inside. "Intersex" describes a person's sex traits. These are part of their body. Some intersex people also identify as transgender.

Jonathan Van Ness is famous for being on Netflix's show *Queer Eye*. Ness identifies as gender nonconforming.

FAST FACT
TRANSGENDER AND INTERSEX PEOPLE SHARE MANY OF THE SAME ISSUES. HOWEVER, EACH GROUP HAS ITS OWN NEEDS TOO.

THE TRANSGENDER COMMUNITY

The transgender community is home to everyone who isn't cisgender.

Not everyone in this community calls themselves transgender. Transgender is an umbrella word for lots of specific identities. Transgender can be a specific identity too.

Some people identify outside the gender binary. They identify as something other than female or male. Many who identify this way call themselves nonbinary.

Some people don't feel any gender at all. Many who feel this way call themselves agender.

Salem X made the agender flag in 2014. Each color stands for a different agender identity.

Janet Mock

Janet Mock started #GirlsLikeUs on Twitter. This hashtag helps transgender women talk about their experiences. Mock is a well-known writer and transgender activist. She's written two books about her life as a transgender woman.

Monica Helms made the trans flag in 1999. She used light pink and blue because those colors are used for baby girls and boys. The white is for all genders and intersex people.

NONBINARY IDENTITIES

Nonbinary is an umbrella word too. It describes all gender identities that aren't entirely female or entirely male. There are many specific identities under the nonbinary umbrella. Some people also identify as just nonbinary.

It's okay to ask someone how they identify if you aren't sure. This way you can know what words they would like you to use for them.

It's not okay to ask someone about their assigned gender. It can be harmful to the person's emotions or their safety.

Kye Rowan made the nonbinary flag in 2014. Yellow, white, and purple stand for different nonbinary identities. Black stands for agender identities.

PRONOUNS AND GENDER

Pronouns are words that identify a person. Pronouns are connected to gender in many languages. In English, "she/her" pronouns are seen as female. "He/him" pronouns are seen as male. Many transgender people change their pronouns.

Sam Smith is a British singer. They came out as nonbinary in March 2019. They began using "they/them" pronouns later that year.

THEY / THEM PRONOUNS

Many nonbinary people use "they/them" pronouns. These words aren't connected to a gender. Some people use other pronouns.

GENDER EXPRESSION

Your gender expression is how you show the world your gender identity. It's what you do on the outside. This can be done through the words you use for yourself, such as a label for your identity. It can be your pronouns and even your name.

You can express gender through your style, like your clothes and hair. You can show it through how you speak and move. You may find certain activities that help you express your gender.

Gender expression can be part of changing gender roles. Flappers were a group of women in the 1920s. They dressed and acted in ways women weren't supposed to.

Some people change how their body looks to better express their gender. Some make their chests look smaller and flatter. This is called binding. Some may use pads to change the shape of their chest, legs, or butt. This is called padding.

Teenagers and adults may choose to change their bodies forever with **hormone** therapy or surgery. These are called gender-**affirming** changes.

Christine Jorgensen was the first known American to have gender-affirming surgeries. She became famous after her surgery.

DRAG AND GENDER

Drag is an art form that plays with society's ideas about gender. Drag is a **performance** for some artists. It's a way to express gender for other artists. For some, it's both! People of all genders take part in drag.

Drag is part of queer culture. The word "queer" is a very big umbrella. It can describe a person's sexuality. Your sexuality is who you are **attracted** to. "Queer" can also describe gender identity. However, gender identity and sexuality are different things.

KINGS AND QUEENS

Artists who dress as women are called drag queens. Most drag queens are gay men. Artists who dress as men are called drag kings. Many drag kings are queer women. Anyone can be a drag queen or king, though.

FAST FACT

THE WORD "DRAG" GOES ALL THE WAY BACK TO THE 1800s! IT WAS USED FOR MALE ACTORS WHO WORE WOMEN'S DRESSES. THEY WERE PERFORMERS.

RuPaul is a famous drag queen and musician. He has a show called *RuPaul's Drag Race*. This show has made drag even more popular.

A HISTORY OF PRIDE

Transgender people and drag artists were grouped together for a long time. In the 1990s, it became clear these groups were different. Transgender people are a gender other than their assigned label. Many drag artists are cisgender. Most drag artists have queer sexualities. Many transgender people identify as straight, or attracted to the opposite gender.

Each group in the queer community has its own challenges. They share many challenges too. All of these groups have experienced discrimination. Sadly, this is still happening today.

 **VERIFIED**

To learn more about RuPaul's work, see his website:
www.rupaul.com

Gia Ichikawa is a drag artist. She was on *RuPaul's Drag Race* in 2014. She came out as transgender in 2017.

There is a long history of pride in the transgender community. STAR (Street Transvestite Action Revolutionaries) was one of the first organizations for transgender people in the United States. It was started by Sylvia Rivera and Marsha P. Johnson. They identified as drag queens. They ran a house for transgender kids and drag queens without homes.

Rivera and Johnson were also at the Stonewall **riots**. This was a protest against the police. The police arrested many transgender and queer people.

SYLVIA RIVERA

This picture shows the crowd trying to prevent police from making arrests outside the Stonewall Inn. A statue of Sylvia Rivera and Marsha P. Johnson is being built and will be placed in Greenwich Village.

THE STONEWALL RIOTS

The Stonewall riots began on June 28, 1969. Police arrested people who weren't wearing at least three pieces of "gender-appropriate" clothing. This meant clothing for their assigned gender.

FIGHTING FOR RIGHTS

The Stonewall riots were very important for the transgender community. They were important for the queer community too. Both groups fought even harder for their rights. This fight still continues today.

Many parts of society are still sorted by gender. This includes sports and other activities. It also includes public bathrooms, locker rooms, and dorm rooms. It can even include schools. Transgender people want to be able to go through all parts of life as their gender.

GENDER AND SPORTS

Transgender people face challenges in sports. They aren't always allowed to play as the gender they identify. Many people think it's not fair to let transgender women play with cisgender women. Transgender activists disagree.

FAMOUS TRANSGENDER ATHLETES

MIANNE BAGGER
The first transgender woman to play professional golf.

JAIYAH SAELUA
The first transgender woman to play in the World Cup (soccer).

CHRIS MOSIER
The first transgender man on Team USA. He is a triathlete and duathlete.

CAITLYN JENNER
Jenner is a famous Olympic athlete. She was assigned male at birth. She played sports as a man. She came out as a woman in 2015.

DISCRIMINATION

Workplaces sometimes fire or might not hire someone because they're transgender. Transgender people in the United States are twice as likely to not find work than cisgender people. They're also twice as likely to live in **poverty**.

They may not be able to pay for housing. Transgender people are sometimes kicked out of their homes. They are often refused housing too. One in five transgender people in the United States experiences homelessness.

INTERSECTIONAL ISSUES

Transgender people of color are the most at risk. This is especially true for black transgender people. A study from 2015 in the United States found these facts:

- 42% of black transgender people experience homelessness.

- 38% of black transgender people live in poverty.

- Black transgender people are much more likely to be accepted by their families.

Gwendolyn Ann Smith started Transgender Day of Remembrance in 1999. It's a day to remember transgender people who died from violence. Smith started it to remember her friend Rita Hester.

VIOLENCE AGAINST THE COMMUNITY

There is also violence against the transgender community. This especially affects transgender people of color. At least 25 transgender or gender-nonconforming people were killed in 2019. Most of those killed were people of color.

PROTECTING THE TRANSGENDER COMMUNITY

The government protects some groups that are discriminated against. One way is with the Civil Rights Act of 1964. This protected the rights of people of color. It also has a part called Title VII. This is about workplace rights. It protects people of all sexes.

Later, transgender people were included in this group. President Obama signed the Fair Pay and Safe Workplaces order in 2014. This was an executive order. It protected transgender and queer people at work.

WHAT ARE EXECUTIVE ORDERS?

Issuing an executive order is one of the president's powers. It acts like a law while the president is in office. Future presidents can end it.

TRANSGENDER ORGANIZATIONS

International

- International Foundation for Gender Education
- GATE
- World Professional Association for Transgender Health
- Transgender Europe

India

- Sahodari Foundation

United Kingdom

- All About Trans
- Trans Media Watch
- The Gender Trust

Australia

- Transgender Victoria

Taiwan

- Taiwan TG Butterfly Garden

United States

- Transgender Law Center
- Trans Student Equality Resources
- Sylvia Rivera Law Project
- National Center for Transgender Equality

Zimbabwe

- GALZ

President Obama wrote guides on how schools should protect people of all sexes. His guides included transgender students. President Trump ended this protection.

STAYING STRONG

People born between 1996 and 2004 are called Generation Z. It's called Gen Z for short. This group has a wider range of gender identities than other age groups before it. Over a third of Gen Z knows someone who uses "they/them" pronouns.

Society will continue to change. That's good news for the transgender community. We are headed to a future that accepts all genders.

✓ VERIFIED

In 2017, the first transgender person appeared on the cover of National Geographic. Avery Jackson is part of Gen Z. For more information about the January 2017 edition, visit: https://www.nationalgeographic.com/magazine/2017/01/

Many people are already accepting of transgender communities. All of us, no matter the age, must work to make the future world a safe and understanding place for everyone.

GLOSSARY

affirm: To show or express a strong belief in something.

ambiguous: Capable of being understood in more than one way.

assign: To give a particular quality, value, or identity to.

attraction: Being romantically or sexually interested in someone.

challenge: Something that is hard to do.

chromosome: The part of a cell that contains the genes that control how an animal or plant grows and what it becomes.

colonization: When one culture takes control over another culture.

culture: The beliefs and ways of life of a certain group of people.

discrimination: Treating a group of people unfairly.

hormone: A natural or added substance produced in the body that controls the way the body develops.

identification: Papers that show who a person is.

identity: Who someone is.

performance: A public presentation.

poverty: The state of being poor.

riot: A large group of people behaving in a wild way.

role: A part or function.

spectrum: A wide range of different possibilities.

trait: A quality that makes a person or thing different from others.

INDEX